City Mouse Hop!

City Mouse Hop!

Bonnie Tarbert

Bonnie Tarbert

"City mouse in the house!" shouts the dad to Henry dog. It's another day about Mousie's food blog.

Free loading Mousie was again
enjoying his life of luxury:
vegetable soup and under the toaster
oven bread crumb mess skulduggery.

**Defying all attempts
of being caught,
he's smart and strong -
a real journey fought.**

Not my
bone!

Mazes of mouse trap
hotels filled with feasts -
landmines of peanut butter and
cheese couldn't contain this beast.

Chocolate bars of every kind were sprawled out to gain his attention. He'll eat though walls and refrigerator wiring to reach his destination.

When Henry questioned
Mousie how he had
managed to escape every catch,
Mousie sat right up and felt
amazed that someone noticed
his skills to resist a latch.

Zoom, zoom!

"Well you see, it's not my nose's sinus infection as you would think."
I know real comforts that are soothing such as my back's furry mink."

Itchy, Scratchy!

"Those mouse trap hotels aren't relaxing like
the blankets in the playroom tent.
I'd rather grab a crumb and itch my back on
that fuzz with my stubby knees bent."

"I enjoy my time listening to Mrs. Belle singing
while she cooks every meal.
I imagine all the amazing treats she drops
from her stirring spoon with appeal."

Mrs. Belle sings in the kitchen some great tunes.
Those words float in the air
alongside zestful fumes.
She sings to me just as happy as can be.

"If you're hungry in your tummy
and you want something yummy -
I've got something savory, cravory,
and deliciously flavory."

"I don't want to leave this home
only to find another that
doesn't have a master cook."

"Mousie, the cafe next door has a coastal menu so you might want to look."

Baltimore Cafe

Mrs. Belle thinks your
chattering peeps are so adorable.
She needs to make room for the baby.
That's why you are so deplorable.

"I promise that I won't be a problem -
I can help cook, clean, and
change those diapers.
I can scoot across the floor to clean
with wet cloth wipers."

"Not only can I do your household chores,
I'm great with tools, and can build
a new mouse door."

" I'm going to chat with Mrs. Belle -
I hope it goes perfectly swell."

Woof, woof,
it's yummy food
here!

Mrs. Belle sings in the kitchen some great tunes.
Those words float in the air
alongside zestful fumes.
She sings to me just as happy as can be.

"If you're hungry in your tummy
and you want something yummy -
I've got something savory, cravory,
and deliciously flavory."

Mrs. Belle makes a decision -
it's something for your mission.
"Since you're earning your stay,
you really must not pay.
Your ambition is delightful and
we enjoy your heart,
you're welcome to stay forever so
you must not part."

CPSIA information can be obtained
at www.ICGtesting.com
Printed in the USA
BVHW020551170922
647274BV00002B/13